LIFE IN THE DEEP SEA

LIFE IN THE DEEP SEA

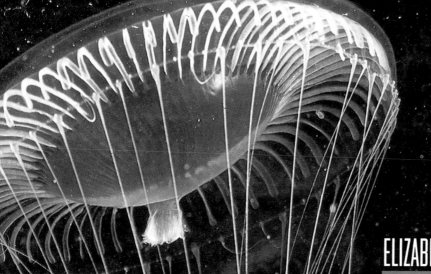

ELIZABETH TAYNTOR GOWELL

A First Book

Franklin Watts
A Division of Grolier Publishing
New York London Hong Kong Sydney
Danbury, Connecticut

For Julia
The author would like to thank Dr. Gene Carl Feldman, Oceanographer at NASA Goddard Space Flight Center, for his technical review of the manuscript.

Interior Design: Kathleen Santini
Photographs:©: Alice Alldredge: 16; Bruce Russell: 40; Corbis-Bettmann: 10, 13, 53 (UPI), 9, 51; John Moore: 32, 33; Norbert Wu Photography: cover, 3 (Chris Parks/Mo Yung Productions), 25 (Peter Parks/Mo Yung Productions), 22, 31, 35, 36, 37; North Wind Picture Archives: 49; Peter Girguis: 24, 43; Photo Researchers: 46 (Bud Lehnhausen), 20 (Peter Ryan/Scripps/SPL), 14 (Tom Van Sant/Geosphere Project/Planetary Visions/SPL), 28 (Dr. Paul A. Zahl); Photri-Microstock: 18, 38; Shana Goffredi: 45; Visuals Unlimited: 27 (Alex Kerstitch); Wildlife Conservative Society, Headquartered at the Bronx Zoo: 6; Woods Hole Oceanographic Institution: 12 (Rod Catanach), 19.

Visit Franklin Watts on the Internet at:
http://publishing.grolier.com

Library of Congress Cataloging-in-Publication Data

Gowell, Elizabeth Tayntor
    Life in the deep sea / by Elizabeth Tayntor Gowell.
        p.   cm. — (A first book)
    Includes bibliographical references and index.
    Summary: Presents a history of deep sea exploration as well as a description of the landscape and life found there.
        ISBN: 0-531-20391-3 (lib. bdg.   0-531-15957-4 (pbk.)
        1. Deep-sea animals — Juvenile literature. 2. Deep-sea biology—
        — Juvenile literature. [1. Marine animals.   2. Marine biology.]
        I. Title. II. Series.
QL125.5.G68   1999
591.77—dc 21   97-52239
                                                                                      CIP
                                                                                      AC

Contents

William Beebe sits atop the bathysphere. Next to him is the cable tha...

1
THE HISTORY OF DEEP-SEA EXPLORATION

It was 1930. William Beebe and his diving partner, Otis Barton, prepared for the journey of a lifetime. They were about to be lowered deep into the ocean off the coast of Bermuda, an island in the Atlantic Ocean. With only a cable to return them to the surface, a *bathysphere* carrying Beebe and Barton descended hundreds of feet into the ocean. Except for the light made by fish, jellyfish, squid, and *plankton* that passed the bathysphere's portholes, the explorers were surrounded by darkness.

On that first dive in 1930, Beebe and Barton reached a maximum depth of 1,426 feet (428 m). Two years later, they descended to 2,200 feet (670 m). In 1934, they reached 3,028 feet (908 m)—more than half a mile below the ocean's surface! At this depth, the water pressed against the porthole of their primitive *submersible* with 19 tons of pressure. "There was no possible chance of being drowned," Beebe later wrote. "The first few drops [of water] would have shot through our flesh and bone like steel bullets."

THE CHALLENGE OF THE DEEP

Although people have been sailing across the ocean's surface for thousands of years, most of what is known about the world beneath the waves has been learned only in the past century. Modern *oceanography,* the study of the oceans, is a relatively new science. It began in 1872 with the voyage of the British ship, HMS *Challenger.*

This 4 year scientific journey studied every aspect of the world's major oceans—the plant and animal life, the water, and the ocean floor. Using nets, thermometers, bottles, and buckets, the scientists on board the *Challenger* lowered cables from their ship to explore the depths and collect information about the vast, watery wilderness below.

The *Challenger* expedition was successful. The crew's findings contributed to the founding of the four major branches of ocean science: marine biology, submarine geology, chemistry of seawater, and physical oceanography. The crew also collected many deep-sea animals that had never been seen before. Yet, most of the ocean remained unexplored. It was not until scientists were able to travel beneath the waves in submersibles, such as Beebe's bathysphere, that the hidden secrets of the deep sea were revealed.

Oceanographers aboard the British ship HMS Challenger *faced all kinds of weather. It was tough work, but in 4 years this expedition discovered more about the world's oceans than had ever been known before.*

THE DEEPEST DIVE

After William Beebe's record-setting trip in 1934, deep-sea explorers began to make deeper and deeper dives. One of the pioneers in depth exploration was French scientist and inventor Auguste Piccard.

Piccard's efforts resulted in a series of deep-sea submersibles that he called *bathyscaphes* or "deep boats." In January 1960, the most famous of these vessels, the *Trieste,* made history. It reached the deepest point in all the world's

Auguste Piccard, inventor of the deep-sea submersible Trieste, *stands with his son, Jacques. Later, Jacques would pilot* Trieste *to Mariana Trench, the deepest place in all the worlds's oceans.*

oceans—the bottom of the 36,198 foot (11,033 m) Mariana Trench, 7 miles (11 km) beneath the surface of the Pacific Ocean! There, at the bottom of the world, with Piccard's son Jacques as pilot and U.S. Navy Lieutenant Don Walsh as co-pilot, a record was set that may be equaled, but will never be beaten.

MODERN SUBMERSIBLES

Despite its deep diving record, *Trieste* was not well suited for undersea exploration. The submersibles that followed were smaller and easier to steer. They were also equipped with cameras and gear for collecting water specimens, rocks, and sea life.

Today, several deep-sea submersibles can dive deep enough to explore all but the deepest trenches. The Russian submersibles *Mir I* and *Mir II,* the French submersible *Nautile,* and the U.S. Navy's *Sea Cliff,* can dive to a depth of 3.7 miles (6 km). The most recently built diving submersible is the Japanese *Shinkai 6500,* which can reach depths of 21, 325 feet (6,500 m).

Although it holds no depth records, perhaps the most famous deep-sea submersible is *Alvin*. This small white mini-sub, owned by the Woods Hole Oceanographic Institution (WHOI) on Cape Cod, Massachusetts, can dive to 14,764 feet (4,500 m). *Alvin* has been used to study undersea volcanoes, deep-sea hot springs, and all kinds of deep-sea life.

Alvin, *a deep-sea submersible operated by Woods Hole Oceanographic Institution, has been used to make many exciting deep-sea discoveries.*

THE POWER OF REMOTE CONTROL

Scientist Robert Ballard, a former WHOI investigator, has probably spent more time in submersibles than anyone else alive. Today he believes that the future of deep-sea exploration depends on small remote control systems like those he used in 1985 to find the lost cruise ship *Titanic*. A towed camera system called *Argo* was used to locate the *Titanic*, and a small remote-controlled robot, called *Jason Jr.* was used to explore the wreck. *Jason Jr.* is so small, it can venture into spaces submersibles can't reach!

Because they are small and carry no crew, *Jason Jr., Argo,* and other remote control vehicles are safer and less expensive to use than submersibles with pilots. Remote control vehicles can also go deeper than the piloted submersibles currently in operation.

On March 24, 1995, the Japanese remote control deep-diving vehicle *Kaiko,* meaning "trench," became the second vehicle to touch down in Challenger Deep at the bottom of the Mariana Trench. No one was aboard, but *Kaiko*'s cameras recorded the event while scientists controlled the expedition from the safety of the surface.

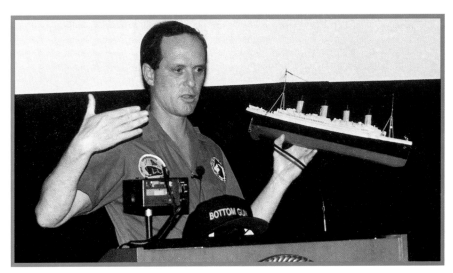

Oceanographer Robert Ballard, a pioneer in modern exploration, describes his deep-sea discovery of the wreckage of the Titanic.

Earth is the ocean planet, but scientists know more about space than about the deep-sea.

2
LANDSCAPE OF THE DEEP-SEA

The deep sea is the largest *habitat* on Earth. Nearly 75 percent of our planet's surface is covered by ocean, and 90 percent of the ocean is more than 1,000 feet (300 m) deep.

Scientists divide the oceans into zones based on depth and available light. The sunlit surface waters are called the *photic zone.* In this zone, which extends from the surface to a depth of about 500 feet (150 m), the sun provides ocean plants with enough energy to survive.

As light penetrates the ocean water, some of it is absorbed, making it difficult for the plants below the photic zone to survive. This middle area of the ocean, is called the *twilight zone.* From 500 to 1,000 feet (150 to 300 m), any light that is still visible gradually fades into complete darkness. Without plants, food is scarce for the many animals that live in the twilight zone. Most of these animals migrate up to the photic zone to feed at night.

Beneath the twilight zone is the deep sea—one of the toughest places to live on Earth. The water is just a few degrees above freezing, it is always dark, and the pressure is intense. Imagine the weight of an elephant pressing down on every square inch of your body. That's how much weight pushes against objects 1,000 feet (300 m) below the surface.

A few *predators* feed on their neighbors in this harsh world, but most deep-sea animals are *scavengers.* They live on *marine snow,* the remains of dead animals and bits of leftover food that drift down from above. Scientists estimate that only 1 percent of the food produced by plants at the surface of the ocean reaches the bottom of the deep sea.

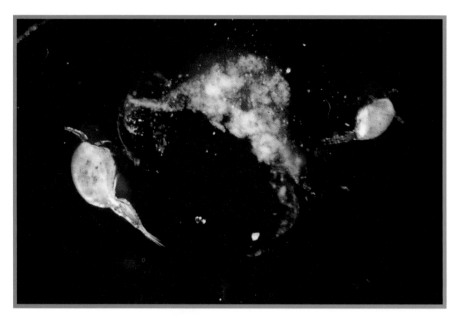

Marine snow is an important source of food for most deep-sea animals.

16

DEEP-SEA MOUNTAINS AND TRENCHES

If you could pull a plug and drain all the water from the oceans, you would see a landscape as dramatic and varied as any found on land. Beneath the ocean's surface are mountain ranges, valleys, deep canyons, and vast plains. There are even undersea volcanoes!

One of the most important features of the ocean landscape is the 46,000 mile (74,000 km) long mid-ocean ridge. At its center lies a giant valley as deep as the Grand Canyon. In this valley, Earth's rocky *crust* is cracking and splitting apart. As it splits, *molten rock* from Earth's core moves toward the surface. When the molten rock hardens, new seafloor is created—but very slowly. Scientists estimate that the seafloor widens about 2 to 7 inches (5 to 18 cm) each year.

Most of the mountains in the mid-ocean ridge are hidden beneath the ocean's surface, but a few of the highest peaks rise above sea level and form islands. The tallest peak rises 27,000 feet (8,000 m) from the seafloor. It is almost as tall as Mount Everest, the highest mountain on land.

The deepest areas on the ocean floor are the deep-sea trenches. The deepest trench of all is the Mariana Trench, located in the Pacific Ocean east of the Philippines. The deepest part of the trench, the Challenger Deep, was not discovered until 1951. As you learned earlier, it is almost 7 miles (11 km) below the ocean's surface. You could sink Mount Everest in the

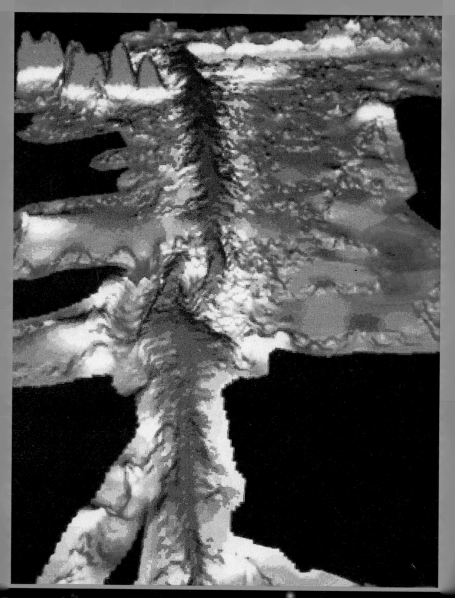

This computer-generated image shows the highest points of a portion of the mid-ocean ridge in red. The tall, red peaks at the top of the

Mariana and it would still be 7,000 feet (2,100 m) below the surface. The deepest ocean trench in the Atlantic, the Puerto Rico Trench, lies 28,374 feet (8,648 m) beneath the surface.

DEEP-SEA HOT SPRINGS

In 1977, scientists exploring the ocean floor in *Alvin,* the deep-sea submersible, made an amazing discovery. In icy cold water, more than 1 mile (1.6 km) beneath the surface of the Pacific Ocean, fountains of hot liquid flowed out of the ocean floor. It was full of *hydrogen sulfide,* a substance that smells like rotten eggs and is poisonous to most animals. Living around these hot springs were strange animals never before seen—clams as big as footballs, tubeworms as tall as

Imagine a worm that is taller than you! The deep-sea tubeworms found around hydrothermal vents can reach heights of 12 feet (3.7 m).

Hot water full of stinky hydrogen sulfide spews from the rock chimney of a deep-sea hydrothermal vent. Scientists call these vents "black smokers."

basketball players, and more. Amazingly, these bizarre creatures were thriving in the hot chemical bath.

Since that discovery, scientists have found and explored many more deep-sea hot springs or *hydrothermal vents.* At some vents, the hot liquid is as black as smoke. At others, it is milky-white. The color comes from minerals that dissolve in hot water as it flows up through cracks in the seafloor.

Many hydrothermal vents are surrounded by rock formations known as *chimneys*. The chimneys form when the mineral-rich liquid of the hot springs hits the cold ocean water. The mineral particles drop out of the liquid and build the rock chimneys layer upon layer.

One of the great mysteries of the hydrothermal vents is how the deep sea, which has so little food, could support such large groups of animals and other creatures. Scientists discovered that at the deep-sea vents, the *food chain* is based on *bacteria,* instead of on plants. The bacteria use the hydrogen sulfide in the vent liquid to produce food through a process called *chemosynthesis.* The bacteria are then eaten, and the nutrients are passed on to other animals in this sunless food chain.

Scientists have also found animal communities supported by chemosynthesis at deep-sea areas called *seeps.* At these sites, oil and natural gas seep or bubble through cracks in the ocean floor and release hydrogen sulfide. The hydrogen sulfide allows bacteria to grow and the bacteria, in turn, provide energy to the seep communities. Some of the best-known seep communities are located in the Gulf of Mexico, at depths of 1,000 feet (300 m) or more.

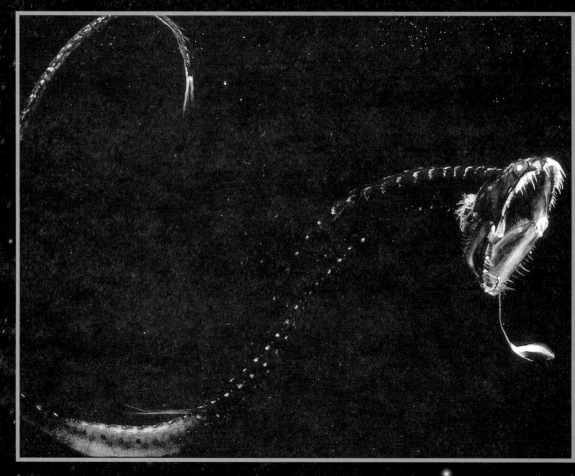

Meet the black sea dragon. Like most deep-sea creatures it is biolu-minescent. Glow-in-the-dark spots line its body from head to tail.

3
LIVING LIGHTS

Sunlight never reaches the deep sea, but explorers who have visited this watery world know that it is not completely dark. Thousands of feet beneath the surface, the darkness sparkles, glows, and flashes with the light of thousands of living stars. Scientists estimate that 75 percent of the animals in the deep ocean can make their own light. The variety of glow-in-the-dark animals in the sea is astonishing.

Except for fireflies, there are few *bioluminescent* animals on land. But in the ocean, scientists have found glowing bacteria, plankton, sea jellies, squid, shrimp, worms, and fish. Each kind of creature displays its living light in its own special way. Some have bright lights on their heads, others on their tails. Some glow all over, while others radiate light in distinct dots of green or bright blue. In some animals, the lights flash on and off, in others they glow continuously.

WHY DO THEY GLOW?

Scientists aren't sure why so many deep-sea dwellers glow in the dark, but self-defense may be one reason. Many animals light up when they are disturbed or in danger. The sudden light may temporarily blind or startle a predator, giving the victim just enough time to make a getaway. One type of deep-sea squid squirts a glowing cloud of ink to distract predators. This may also protect the squid by making it look bigger than it really is. Some animals may light up to draw attention to their attacker.

This bioluminescent squid may use light to startle and confuse its predators. Other deep-sea dwellers use light to attract their prey.

Deep-sea animals may also use bioluminescence to find or attract food. Some deep-sea fish have glowing organs in and around their mouths that may lure other fish. When a smaller animal gets close, these fish snap them up with their sharp teeth. Other fish have bright lights near their eyes. These may be used like headlights to find and capture *prey*.

For animals that live together in groups, like fish or shrimp, body lights may provide signals to nearby animals. At night, shrimplike deep-sea animals called *euphasids* gather in swarms and migrate from the deep ocean to shallower waters in search of food. Red spots of light along their

Euphasids, also called krill, are an important source of food for whales.

sides flash on and off. Scientists think euphasids use these lights to signal one another to stay nearby, but not so close that they bump into one another. Euphasids also have lights on their eye stalks that may be used to search for food.

Small deep-sea animals called *ostracods* release a cloud of blue light when they feel threatened. This may confuse and distract their enemies. At other times, male ostracods flash specific patterns of light as they swim. Scientists aren't sure why ostracods do this. It may be that—like fireflies—ostracods use the flashing light to attract mates.

How Do They Glow?

Deep-sea animals light up with special glow-in-the-dark chemicals. When these chemicals react with other substances, they produce energy in the form of light. In many animals, the glow-in-the-dark chemicals are located in cells that are clustered together into organs called *photophores*. Some photophores are lined with reflective tissue that make the light look brighter. Others are shielded by a layer of black skin.

Many of the fish that glow do not make their own light. Some have glowing bacteria living inside them. The bacteria may be located in the fish's skin or concentrated in sac-like pockets. Since the bacteria glow all the time, the fish usually have some mechanism to hide the glow. Flashlight fish have a special flap of muscle that can be raised and lowered like a window shade to cover the pockets of glowing bacteria be-

Flashlight fish have a pocket of skin filled with glowing bacteria beneath each eye. The fish may use these flashlights to find food in the darkness.

neath their eyes. To confuse predators, flashlight fish use a flash-and-run technique. The "flashlights" may also be used to locate prey.

When two different types of organisms, such as flashlight fish and bacteria, live together, their close association is called *symbiosis.* Each organism benefits. The fish benefits from the light the bacteria make. By living inside the fish, the bacteria are safe from predators. A symbiotic relationship that benefits both types of organisms is called *mutualism.*

Lanternfish live in the depths by day, then migrate to the surface at night in search of food. They have large eyes and glowing spots that may help attract their prey.

4
DEEP-SEA FISH

Many deep-sea fish are monstrous-looking creatures with names to match. Sea dragons, viperfish, black sea devils, and gulper eels are just a few of the strange and fascinating fish that live in the deep ocean. Scientists have learned that the bizarre appearance of some of these deep-sea fish is due to special features designed to help them survive in the ocean's underworld.

LANTERNFISH

Lanternfish are named for the rows of glowing spots on their bellies and sides. Although these fish are only 2 to 6 inches (5 to 15 cm) long, each one has 50 to 80 "glowing lights" that flash as blue as an electric spark. Each species of lanternfish has a different number and pattern of lights. These patterns may help the fish identify others of their own kind. Lanternfish are one of several types of ocean creatures that hover in the depths by day, and migrate to the photic zone at night to feed.

GULPERS AND SWALLOWERS

With so little food in the deep sea, many fish go for days or even weeks between meals.

The gulper eel is a slender fish about 24 inches (60 cm) long. Its most remarkable feature is its enormous mouth. Although it has no teeth, the gulper eel can swallow animals as large—or even larger—than itself. Its stomach expands to let it store, and slowly digest, meals of all sizes. Like many deep-sea dwellers, the gulper eel is black and has tiny eyes that are almost useless in the dark, icy depths.

The black swallower is a close relative of the gulper eel, but it is much longer. This deep-sea predator grows 6 feet (1.8 m) long and has a mouthful of teeth. The tip of its tail has a glowing organ. The bioluminescence patterns found along its back help to identify this species from others within this group of fish.

DEEP-SEA ANGLERFISH

One of the most famous of the deep-sea anglerfish is the black sea devil. This fish has a long fin on its back with a piece of glowing flesh at the end. To attract its prey, the anglerfish dan-

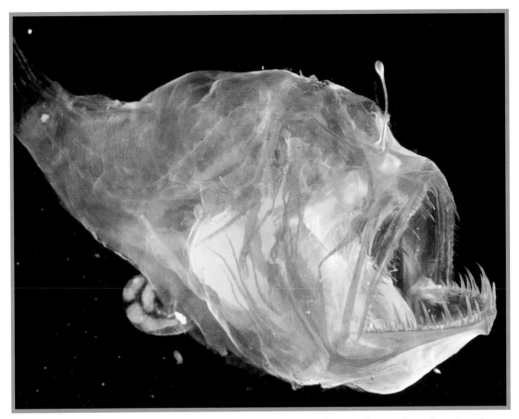

This specimen of a deep sea anglerfish has been cleaned and stained with dye to show bone (red) and cartilage (blue). Look at the sharp teeth and dangling lure on the top of its head.

gles this glowing lure over its own huge mouth. When a small fish or shrimp swims up to investigate, the sea devil traps it with its pointed teeth and swallows its victim whole.

The sea devil has an unusual way of finding a mate. The male anglerfish, which is much smaller than the female,

Lantern sharks are small but fierce. Like wolves, they hunt in groups, surrounding a larger animal, then closing in for the kill.

grasps its mate with its jaws and holds on until it becomes permanently fused to the female's body. This behavior ensures that when the female is ready to lay eggs, the male is at her side to fertilize them.

Female anglerfish maybe more than 36 inches (90 cm) long and weigh more than 20 pounds (9 kg). The males, however, are only 4 inches (10 cm) long and weigh less than 5 pounds (2 kg).

GLOW-IN-THE-DARK SHARKS

The thought of sharks scares almost everyone. But imagine meeting a glowing shark thousands of feet below the ocean's surface! Lantern sharks, also called green dogfish, have photophores on their bellies that cast an eerie green glow. This bioluminescent light can be seen from 10 to 12 feet (3 to 4 m) away. One researcher who was studying a captured lantern shark in a dark room reported that its entire body, from nose to tail, glowed with a pale green light.

Like most of the sharks discovered in the deep sea, lantern sharks are fairly small—only about 18 inches (45 cm) long. Scientists think these small sharks hunt in packs. First, they surround a deep-sea animal that is larger than they are, like a squid or octopus. Then all the members of the pack move in and attack with their razor-sharp teeth. The glowing green lights on the bellies of lantern sharks, may help these predators stay together during an attack and keep them from biting one another in their feeding frenzy.

Another small but fierce deep-sea shark is the cookie-cutter shark. This little hunter uses its sharp teeth to nip round, cookie-shaped bites of flesh from larger animals. Like lantern sharks, cookie-cutter sharks glow in the dark. In fact, some scientists call them the brightest of all sharks. There are photophores all over this shark's belly that glow with a bright green light. Scientists think the cookie-cutter shark may use these lights to attract its prey. Then, when a larger animal gets close, the smaller shark lunges toward it and takes a quick bite.

THE TRIPOD FISH

The tripod fish has a tall, slender, long fin and two side fins that hang down below its body to form the three legs of its "tripod." These fins hold the fish steady as it waits for food above the ocean floor. Because it has tiny eyes, the tripod fish uses its sense of touch, to find its prey in the darkness of the deep sea. Long *antenna*-like fins hang above the fish's mouth. When a small fish or shrimp bumps into these fins, the tripod fish snaps up its dinner.

The tripod fish can use its stilt-like fins to hold itself just above the sea floor.

THE BLACK VIPERFISH

The viperfish is about 10 to 12 inches (25 to 30 cm) long. It has large eyes, a big mouth, and fang-like teeth that curve backward to trap its prey. Some types of viperfish have a long fin spine that curves forward over its head like a fishing pole. The end of the spine dangles above the viper's mouth and acts like a lure. Scientists think the viperfish's spine may attract lanternfish, squid, and other deep-sea creatures.

A little hatchetfish is no match for the fang-like teeth and powerful jaws of a viperfish.

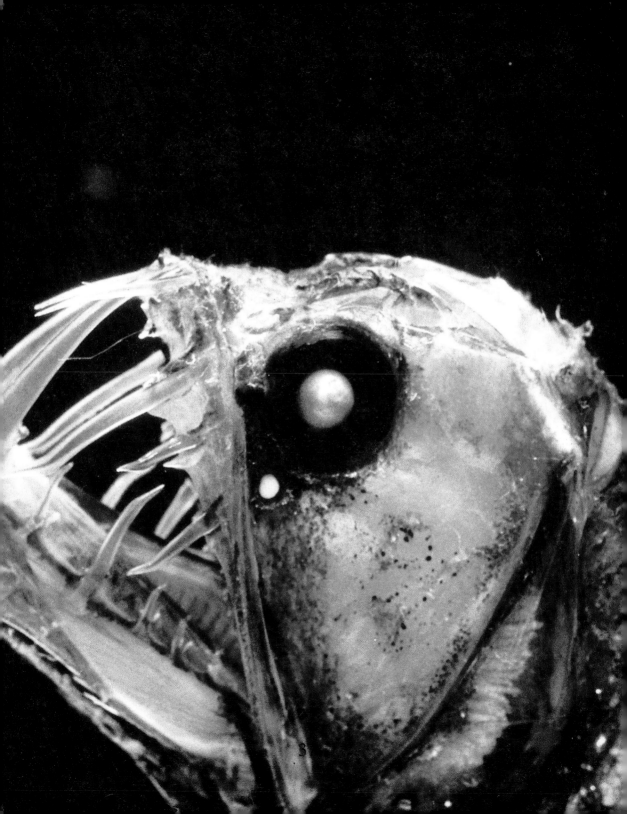

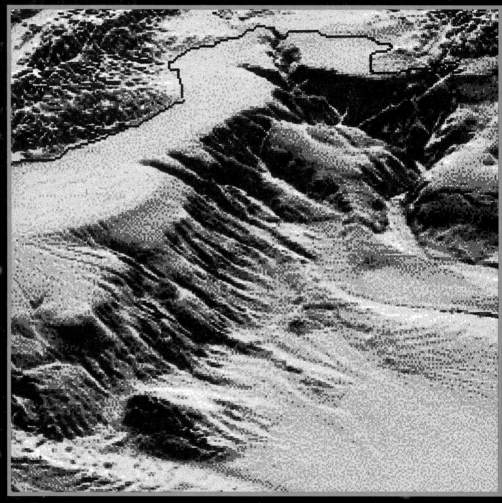

Mud and silt flow down the edge of the continents to cover the abyssal plain. Scientists once thought this plain was a muddy desert. Now they are discovering that it is an ocean region rich with life.

5
THE OCEAN FLOOR

If you moved along the floor of the deep ocean in a submersible, you would see hundreds and hundreds of miles of flat plains covered with mud. At first glance, the *abyssal plain* looks like a pretty boring place. But upon closer investigation, this part of the seafloor is a habitat full of surprises.

The ocean floor around the continents is covered with sand and silt. This material has been carried from the land by rivers, then distributed by ocean currents. Farther offshore, the bottom is covered with a blanket of deep-sea "ooze" made up of the skeletons of trillions of tiny ocean plants and animals. In some areas, the ooze is made up of the skeletons of single-celled creatures known as *foraminifera.* In other areas, it consists of the skeletons of microscopic creatures called *diatoms* or the shells of tiny swimming snails called pteropods.

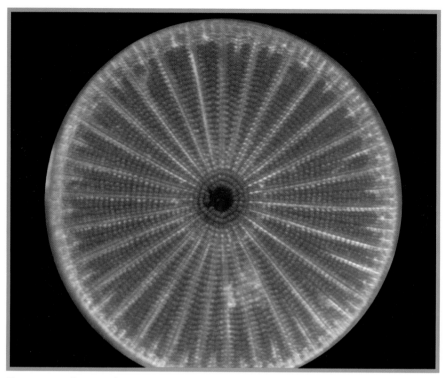

In some places the ocean bottom is covered with a thick blanket of ooze, created by the skeletons of trillions of microscopic plants called diatoms.

Scientists estimate that even with the constant rain of plant and animal remains from above, deep-ocean sediments build up more slowly than dust in your bedroom. It takes about 2,000 years to deposit 1 inch (2.5 cm) of sediment.

Yet, over millions of years, the abyssal plains have been covered by layers of ooze and mud that are now 900 to 1,600 feet (300 to 500 m) deep. Scientists have found that by studying these layers, they can learn a lot about changes in Earth's climate and other events that have effected life on the planet over the past 100 million years.

To study deep-sea sediments, scientists drill into the ocean floor and remove long tubes full of mud and ooze in samples called cores. Then they "read" the sediment layers. In a sample collected recently in the Atlantic Ocean, scientists found a thin streak of brownish-red mud sandwiched between the more common layers of gray and green.

Scientists believe that this streak was deposited more than 67 million years ago when a giant *meteorite* collided with Earth. The meteorite is estimated to have been 10 to 20 miles (16 to 32 km) wide. The collision was so catastrophic that many scientists believe it caused the extinction of the dinosaurs. That thin brownish-red streak in the deep-sea sediments is all that remains of this giant fireball today.

SPINELESS WONDERS

Many scientists are surprised at the wealth of animal life found on the muddy seafloor. Until about 100 years ago, most scientists believed that nothing lived in that dark, cold wasteland. Now scientists are discovering that the numbers and types of animals found on the bottom of the deep sea may be as great as those found on land. Although many of these deep-sea animals are small and strange-looking, scientists believe they are a critical link in the deep-sea food chain.

Many of the species found living on the floor of the deep sea are *invertebrates,* animals without backbones. Sponges, sea stars, crabs, and worms are all found more than 1 mile (1.6 km) beneath the surface. Although they are related to familiar animals found along the ocean's edge, the deep-sea varieties have developed some unusual features. These features are special *adaptations* that help them survive in the depths.

Some of the most beautiful deep-sea invertebrates are the glass sponges. These animals have sharp, fiberglass-like skeletons shaped like vases or tulips. Like their shallow-water relatives, deep-sea sponges are *filter feeders.* They live on tiny particles of food that are carried to them on the flowing ocean currents. Sometimes, animals live inside these deep-sea sponges. The Venus flower basket sponge is often home to a pair of shrimp that find protection within the sponge's skeleton. Skeletons of this sponge are given as wedding presents in Japan.

Millions of worms live on the ocean floor, but they are rarely seen. Most lie buried within the mud and ooze. Like most deep-sea bottom dwellers, they are scavengers. With tentacles extended, they reach out from the mud to capture their diet of marine snow.

The most frequently observed animal on the floor of the deep ocean is the sea cucumber. Sea cucumbers are related to sea stars. They move about with rows of feet that are extended and withdrawn by pumping water in and out. Most

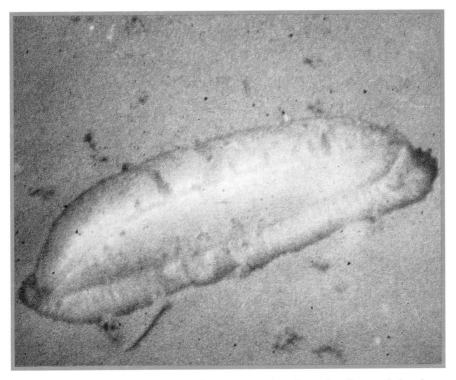

Sea cucumbers are the most often seen animal on the floor of the deep sea. While most of these invertebrates are about 4 inches (10 cm) long, some can be as large as 18 inches (45 cm).

sea cucumbers use their feet to burrow and plow through the mud. Like deep-sea garbage recyclers they digest the bits of food hidden within the mud and ooze.

While most deep-sea cucumbers are about 4 inches (10 cm) long, some grow up to 18 inches (45 cm). Shallow-water types are usually black or brown, but deep-sea cucumbers can be black, red, orange, or purple. The reasons for the colors are not known. Some deep-sea cucumbers shine with a bright blue light when they are touched. Perhaps they use this light to startle predators or to identify their territory to other bottom-dwellers.

Deep-sea cucumbers also differ from their coastal cousins in shape. As you might guess from their name, most shallow-water sea cucumbers are shaped like the vegetable cucumbers, with short feet added for crawling. But deep-sea cucumbers have various shapes.

Some deep-sea cucumbers have fleshy extensions that look like tails, *antennae,* or fingers. One of these creatures is so strangely shaped that it looks more like a sea jelly than a sea cucumber. Unlike other deep-sea cucumbers, it swims! Scientists who have observed this unusual creature from submersibles and through underwater cameras believe that it never touches the bottom. Instead, it floats and swims in the water collecting bits of marine snow.

SEA STARS OF THE DEEP

After the sea cucumbers, the most visible animals on the deep ocean floor are the sea stars. The most common sea stars at this depth are the brittle stars. These animals have five slender arms surrounding a round body. The arms are very flexible, and brittle stars use them to slither across the ocean floor. Some brittle stars can even swim for short distances.

With long spidery arms, this deep-sea brittle star slithers quickly along the ocean floor. Its broken arm may have been sacrificed to save it from a hungry predator.

Most brittle stars are small, but some types have arms that are 15 inches (38 cm) long, giving them a total width of almost 33 inches (90 cm). If it is attacked, a brittle star will break off one of its arms to get away. This behavior is one of the reasons for the name "brittle star." Like other sea stars, brittle stars can regrow their lost limbs.

For hundreds of years, the ocean was regarded as a deep, dark, and dangerous place. Even today, there are many things we do not know or understand about this watery world beneath the waves.

6
GIANTS OF THE DEEP

For years, humans saw the ocean only from the surface and feared what creatures might lurk beneath the waves. Stories of imaginary monsters and giant animals of the deep come from all over the world. Fantastic fishes, serpents, and creatures of all shapes and sizes were drawn on early maps to warn explorers and sailors of the dangers they might face. There were few facts, but many legends to explain the mysteries of the seas and the life within them.

Today, thanks to submersibles and remote-control vehicles, our explorations of the ocean have taken us far beneath the surface. We know more about the deep sea than ever before. Sea "monsters" are still sighted from time to time, but most can be explained as floating logs, masses of seaweed, huge whales, or giant squid. There are scientific explanations today for many animals that were once believed to be only

47

imaginary. Scientists have found real animals that are more bizarre than anything ever imagined.

The more we discover, the less real those old legendary sea monsters seem. But can scientists be sure that sea monsters do not exist? Recent discoveries have shown that the deep sea is not an empty desert. It is full of life, and may have enough food to feed a deep-sea giant. How big would this deep-sea giant be? It would probably be too big and too fast to ever be caught by humanmade vehicles. Perhaps it would spot our submersibles coming long before we could see it. But maybe someday a deep-sea camera will identify such a monster. Until then, we have only some ancient sea stories, their modern explanations, and a few unsolved mysteries of the deep ocean.

SEA SERPENTS

Have you ever seen an old map with a sea serpent on it? This legendary creature looks like a snake, has the head of a dragon, and is covered with scales. One giant sea serpent was believed to be so large that it circled the globe.

In stories told hundreds of years ago, sea serpents attacked ships and killed sailors. In modern tales, they are reported to be secretive creatures.

Are sea serpents real? Probably not. Most sea serpents have been sighted along stormy coastlines in fog or rain and can probably be explained as floating logs. But there is at

In ancient legends, sea serpents were one of the most feared sea monsters.

least one deep-sea fish that looks like the strange sea serpents of legend.

Imagine a fish as long as a school bus! The oarfish reaches a length of 50 feet (15 m) and may have been responsible for some sea serpent sightings. It looks like a long ribbon of silver topped by a bright red fin. The fin begins as a crest at the fish's head and runs down its back. Like legendary sea serpents, oarfish are sometimes seen swimming at the surface. A few have been washed up on shore. Oarfish are real, but very rare, and scientists know little about them.

MOBY DICK

Perhaps the most famous of the American sea monsters was the great white sperm whale Moby Dick—part fact and part fiction. Sperm whales are huge. They can grow to be 60 feet (18 m) long and weigh 50 to 60 tons, but they are not monsters. In fact, for hundreds of years, these giants have had more to fear from people than people have had to fear from them. Whales of all kinds have been hunted and killed by the thousands for their oil and meat, but whales do not hunt people.

Sperm whales feed on squid. On one breath of air, a sperm whale can dive 2 miles (3.2 km) deep and spend more than an hour underwater. Most of the squid caught by sperm whales are bite-sized. But sometimes these whales go after big prey. They hunt the "sea monster" called the Kraken.

THE KRAKEN

For hundred of years, one of the real monsters of the deep sea seemed too strange to be true. Although there had been sightings of Kraken, or giant squid, since the 1500s, it was not until the late 1800s that this creature of Danish legend became a creature of fact. Unfortunately, scientists have never seen these magnificent creatures alive in their native habitat. All we know about giant squid comes from the study of dead squid that have

*The great white whale of Herman Melville's novel **Moby Dick** was a fearful monster that attacked ships and killed men.*

occasionally washed up on shore or from the remains of squid found in the stomach or vomit of sperm whales.

Still, scientists know that these relatives of clams and octopuses are real and can reach amazing lengths of almost 60 feet (18 m). Like all squid, giant squid have ten arms. Two of these arms have long tentacles with suction cups near their tips, and are used to catch and hold prey. There are many exciting accounts of sperm whales battling with giant squid. There are also accounts of whales that have been scarred by the tentacles of giant squid. The mouth of a giant squid is located in the center of its tentacles. It is hard and sharp, like the beak of a parrot, perfect for ripping and crushing prey.

Scientists have few clues as to what these giants eat, but whatever their diet is, squid are well-designed to find their food in the darkness of the deep sea. Giant squid have eyes that are larger than volleyballs—more than 18 inches (46 cm) wide. The largest eyes of any animals on Earth. Surely, these amazing animals are one of the ocean's greatest predators.

THE SEARCH FOR TRUTH CONTINUES

As scientists explore the deep sea, each expedition brings new discoveries. Today, instead of fear, we are filled with curiosity to learn more and more about real sea monsters that may dwell in the ocean's depths.

The development of improved deep-sea exploration equipment like the robotic camera *Jason Jr.* has allowed scientists to explore more of the deep sea than ever before. In the future, even more radical inventions are expected to open new windows to our understanding of the deep sea.

One of these inventions is the crittercam, a video camera designed to be attached to an animal and follow its movements. Attached to the back of a whale, a crittercam could

The robotic camera Jason Jr. *explores the wreck of the* Titanic. *Technolological advances like underwater robots have opened up new opportunities for deep-sea exploration.*

give scientists a "whale's eye tour" of the deep ocean. Where would this tour take us? What would we see? If there are sea "monsters" to be found, inventions like crittercam may find them. If scientists ever come face to face with a giant squid, it just might be through a video camera, riding on the back of a whale.

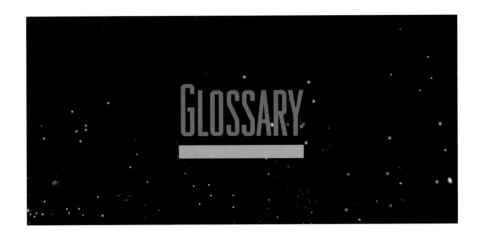

abyssal plain—any of the great flat areas of deep ocean floor.

adaptation—a special characteristic that helps an animal survive in its habitat.

antenna—a slender feeler located on the head of some animals. It contains sense organs.

bacteria—microscopic single-celled organisms.

bathyscaphe—one of the first submersibles able to dive with a pilot and crew to the floor of the deep ocean and return to the surface under their own power.

bathysphere—a metal ball or sphere lowered on a cable from a ship for deep sea diving.

bioluminescent—able to produce light.

chemosynthesis—the process by which microorganisms use energy produced during chemical reactions to produce food from carbon dioxide and water.

chimney—a tall column of solidified minerals on the ocean floor.

crust—Earth's outermost layer.

crustacean—a creature that has no backbone, a hard outer shell, and usually lives in the water. Examples include lobsters, shrimp, and crabs.

diatom—a small creature that lives in watery environments. Diatoms are a common component of plankton.

euphasid—a small shrimplike creature that lives in the ocean.

filter feeder—an organism that obtains food by filtering small particles from relatively large volumes of water.

food chain—a series of organisms that pass food energy from one to another through predation. The smallest organisms in the chain are eaten by larger organisms, which are then eaten by still larger organisms.

foraminifer—a small creature that lives in the ocean.

habitat—the place and natural conditions in which a plant or animal lives.

hydrogen sulfide—a chemical that is toxic to most animals, but used by some bacteria to make food in a process known as chemosynthesis.

hydrothermal vent—a place on the ocean floor where hot, chemical-filled water flows up through cracks in Earth's crust.

invertebrate—a creature without a backbone.

marine snow—the remains of plants and animals that drift down from the sunlit surface waters of the ocean to the depths. Marine snow is the base of most deep-sea food chains.

meteorite—a piece of rock or metal from space that strikes Earth's surface.

mid-ocean ridge—a huge undersea mountain range.

molten rock—rock that has been softened by heat within Earth's mantle.

mutualism—a form of symbiosis that benefits both organisms.

oceanography—the science that deals with the oceans and the living things in them.

ostracod—a small, seed-shaped animal with two shells. Ostracods live in water.

photic zone—the area of the ocean where there is enough sunlight for plants to survive.

photophore—a glowing organ that contains light-producing chemicals.

plankton—a tiny animal or plant that lives in water.

predator—an animal that eats other animals.

pressure—the force produced by pressing on something.

prey—an animal that is eaten by other animals.

scavenger—an animal that feeds on decaying material.

seep—an area of the sea floor where hydrogen sulfide is released by the seeping or bubbling of oil or natural gas up through the ocean bottom.

submersible—a vehicle designed for underwater exploration.

symbiosis—the close association of two different organisms, in which one or both benefit from the relationship.

twilight zone—the area of the ocean below the sunlit photic zone and above the zone of total darkness.

RESOURCES

BOOKS

Ellis, Richard. *Deep Atlantic: Life, Death and Exploration in the Abyss.* New York: Alfred A. Knopf, 1996.

Ganeri, Anita. *The Oceans Atlas.* New York: Dorling Kindersly, 1994.

Kovacs, Deborah and Kate Madin. *Beneath Blue Waters: Meetings with Remarkable Deep Sea Creatures.* New York: Viking, 1996.

Taylor, Leighton and Norbert Wu (photographer). *Creeps from the Deep: Life in the Deep Sea.* San Francisco: Chronicle Books, 1997.

MAGAZINE ARTICLE

Pollard, Jean Ann. "Beebe Takes the Bathysphere." *Sea Frontiers.* August, 1994.

VIDEO

Deep Sea Dive. National Geographic Society, 1993.

ONLINE SITES

The Jason Project describes the expeditions of the remotely operated vehicle *Jason* and deep-sea scientist Robert Ballard. The address is *http://www.jasonproject.org/*

Monterey Bay Aquarium Deep Sea Research describes on-going deep-sea research. It also provides pictures and information about a variety of ocean animals and environments. The address is *http://www.mbayaq.org/atc/atc_ds.htm*

Paul Yancey's Deep Sea is maintained by Paul H. Yancey, a Professor of Biology at Whitman College. This page provides research updates and photographs of deep-sea animals. It also has good links to other deep-sea sites. The address is *http://www.bmi.net/yancey/*

Deep Submergence Laboratory of the Woods Hole Oceanographic Institution provides information about deep-sea research expeditions and vehicles. The address is *http://www.dsl.whoi.edu*

INDEX

ABOUT THE AUTHOR

Elizabeth Tayntor Gowell enjoys exploring the ocean and writing about marine life. She is an award winning author and environmental consultant. Ms. Gowell has worked for the New England Aquarium; the Massachusetts Coastal Zone Management Program; and SEACAMP, a marine science education program in the Florida Keys. She has never been deeper than 100 feet (30 m) beneath the ocean surface, but she has always been fascinated by the creatures that dwell in the deep sea. Ms. Gowell lives in the ocean state of Rhode Island with her husband, Jay, and her three children—Emily, Matthew, and Julia.